The Mural Project

ANSEL ADAMS

RUNNING PRESS · PHILADELPHIA, PENNSYLVANIA

Postcard Book is a trademark of Running Press Book Publishers.

Canadian representatives: General Publishing Co., Ltd., 30 Lesmill Road, Don Mills, Ontario M3B 2T6.

9 8 7 6 5 4 3 2
Digit on the right indicates the number of this printing.

ISBN: 1–56138–096–2
Edited by Gregory C. Aaron
Cover design by Toby Schmidt
Interior design by Nancy Loggins
Front cover and title page: *Yellowstone Lake, Mt. Sheridan,* Yellowstone National Park, Wyoming, 1942,
by Ansel Adams. National Archives and Records Administration.
Back cover: *Church, Taos Pueblo, New Mexico, 1942,*
by Ansel Adams. National Archives and Records Administration.

**Images made from copy prints of Ansel Adams photographs.
Reproduced without consent of the Ansel Adams Publishing Rights Trust.**

Printed and bound in the United States by Innovation Printing.

This book may be ordered by mail from the publisher. Please add $2.50 for postage and handling.
But try your bookstore first!
Running Press Book Publishers
125 South Twenty-second Street
Philadelphia, Pennsylvania 19103–4399

MANY ARTISTS CAN pinpoint crucial moments in their creative lives, but few are clearer than the revelation that came to Ansel Adams during a family vacation when he was fourteen. After insistent pleadings from young Ansel, the Adams family traveled to Yosemite National Park. Ansel Adams later remembered that as their bus drew into the park, he was captivated by the park's natural wonders, and the effects of the sunlight on them. The next day, Adams took his first photograph—a landscape of mountains and clouds. The links between the photographer, the American wilderness, and the fantastic light that emanated from it were forged that day and were never broken.

Over the next three decades, Adams became recognized as one of the world's finest photographers. He championed photography as an art form and helped establish the Department of Photography at the Museum of Modern Art in New York. A superb technician, he also developed the Zone System, a set of guidelines for planning exposures. Using these techniques, Adams captured contrasts of light and darkness that reveal the essences of his subjects and are the hallmarks of his sensitive art. To help preserve his beloved wilderness spaces, he served for thirty-seven years on the board of trustees of the Sierra Club.

The photographs in this collection were commissioned from Adams by Secretary of the Interior Harold Ickes and were mostly taken between October, 1941, and September, 1942. The photos were to be used as giant murals of the national park system in the Department of the Interior's museum, but the project was halted by the Second World War and the photos were never used for their original purpose.

For an appreciative public, Adams's photos evoke an earlier, unspoiled time in American history. Through his lens, we can experience the breathtaking, rugged beauty of our nation. Although the photos offer strict reality—the sometimes startling abstract forms and surprising vistas are earthly places within the boundaries of our nation—they also offer a beauty seldom glimpsed in our daily travels.

In Glacier National Park

Montana, 1942

by Ansel Adams (American, 1902–1984).

National Archives and Records Administration.

T h e   M u r a l   P r o j e c t

A   P o s t c a r d   B o o k ™

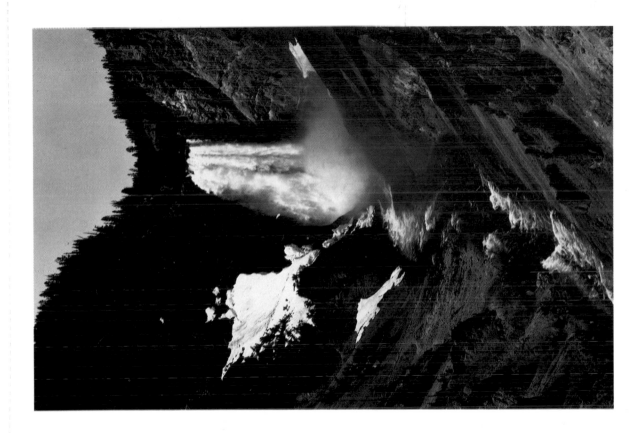

Yellowstone Falls

Yellowstone National Park, Wyoming, 1942

by Ansel Adams (American, 1902–1984).

National Archives and Records Administration.

T h e   M u r a l   P r o j e c t

A   P o s t c a r d   B o o k ™

Saguaros, Saguaro National Monument

Arizona, 1941

by Ansel Adams (American, 1902–1984).

National Archives and Records Administration.

The Mural Project

A Postcard Book ™

Church, Taos Pueblo, New Mexico, 1942

by Ansel Adams (American, 1902–1984).

National Archives and Records Administration.

T h e   M u r a l   P r o j e c t

A   P o s t c a r d   B o o k ™

© 1994 BY RUNNING PRESS BOOK PUBLISHERS

Corn Field, Indian Farm near Tuba City, Arizona, in Rain, 1941

by Ansel Adams (American, 1902–1984).

National Archives and Records Administration.

T h e   M u r a l   P r o j e c t

A   P o s t c a r d   B o o k ™

© 1994 BY RUNNING PRESS BOOK PUBLISHERS

In Glacier National Park

Montana, 1942

by Ansel Adams (American, 1902–1984).

National Archives and Records Administration.

In Glacier National Park

Montana, 1942

by Ansel Adams (American, 1902–1984).

National Archives and Records Administration.

T h e   M u r a l   P r o j e c t

A   P o s t c a r d   B o o k ™

© 1994 BY RUNNING PRESS BOOK PUBLISHERS

Canyon de Chelly

Arizona, 1942

by Ansel Adams (American, 1902–1984).

National Archives and Records Administration.

T h e   M u r a l   P r o j e c t
A   P o s t c a r d   B o o k ™

Grand Teton

Grand Teton National Park, Wyoming, 1942

by Ansel Adams (American, 1902–1984).

National Archives and Records Administration.

T h e   M u r a l   P r o j e c t

A   P o s t c a r d   B o o k ™

Yellowstone Lake, Mt. Sheridan

Yellowstone National Park, Wyoming, 1942

by Ansel Adams (American, 1902–1984).

National Archives and Records Administration.

T h e   M u r a l   P r o j e c t

A   P o s t c a r d   B o o k ™

© 1994 BY RUNNING PRESS BOOK PUBLISHERS

Grand Canyon from S. Rim, 1941

Grand Canyon National Park, Arizona, 1941

by Ansel Adams (American, 1902–1984).

National Archives and Records Administration.

T h e   M u r a l   P r o j e c t

A   P o s t c a r d   B o o k ™

Near Death Valley National Monument

California, 1941

by Ansel Adams (American, 1902–1984).

National Archives and Records Administration.

Zion National Park, 1941

Zion National Park, Utah

by Ansel Adams (American, 1902–1984).

National Archives and Records Administration.

T h e   M u r a l   P r o j e c t

A   P o s t c a r d   B o o k ™

Near Death Valley

Death Valley National Monument, California, 1941

by Ansel Adams (American, 1902–1984).

National Archives and Records Administration.

T h e   M u r a l   P r o j e c t

A   P o s t c a r d   B o o k ™

© 1994 BY RUNNING PRESS BOOK PUBLISHERS

Image made from a copy print of an Ansel Adams photograph. Reproduced without consent of the Ansel Adams Publishing Rights Trust.

Untitled

Mesa Verde National Park, Colorado, 1941

by Ansel Adams (American, 1902–1984)

National Archives and Records Administration.

T h e   M u r a l   P r o j e c t
A   P o s t c a r d   B o o k ™

Acoma Pueblo, New Mexico, 1941

by Ansel Adams (American, 1902–1984).

National Archives and Records Administration.

Church, Acoma Pueblo

New Mexico, 1941

by Ansel Adams (American, 1902–1984).

National Archives and Records Administration.

The Mural Project
A   P o s t c a r d   B o o k ™

Evening, McDonald Lake, Glacier National Park

Montana, 1942

by Ansel Adams (American, 1902–1984).

National Archives and Records Administration.

T h e   M u r a l   P r o j e c t

A   P o s t c a r d   B o o k ™

© 1994 BY RUNNING PRESS BOOK PUBLISHERS

Grand Canyon National Park

Arizona, 1941

by Ansel Adams (American, 1902–1984).

National Archives and Records Administration.

T h e   M u r a l   P r o j e c t
A   P o s t c a r d   B o o k ™

Untitled

Glacier National Park, Montana, 1942

by Ansel Adams (American, 1902–1984).

National Archives and Records Administration.

The Mural Project

A   Postcard   Book ™

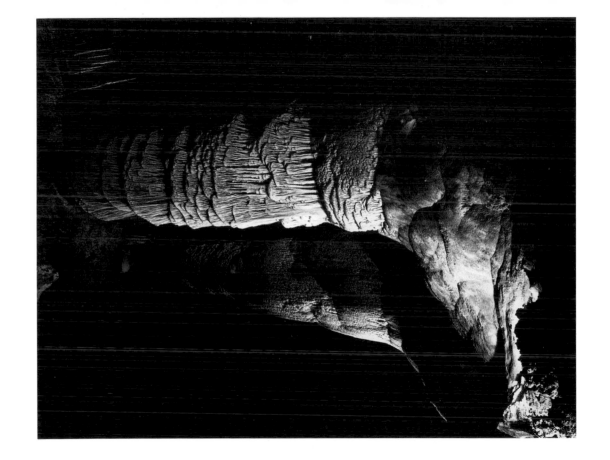

The Giant Dome

Carlsbad Caverns National Park, New Mexico, 1941

by Ansel Adams (American, 1902–1984).

National Archives and Records Administration.

T h e   M u r a l   P r o j e c t

A   P o s t c a r d   B o o k ™

Yellowstone Falls

Yellowstone National Park, Wyoming, 1942

by Ansel Adams (American, 1902–1984).

National Archives and Records Administration.

T h e   M u r a l   P r o j e c t

A   P o s t c a r d   B o o k ™

From Going-to-the-Sun Chalet, Glacier National Park

Montana, 1942

by Ansel Adams (American, 1902–1984).

National Archives and Records Administration.

T h e   M u r a l   P r o j e c t

A   P o s t c a r d   B o o k ™

Canyon de Chelly

Arizona, 1942

by Ansel Adams (American, 1902–1984).

National Archives and Records Administration.

T h e   M u r a l   P r o j e c t

A   P o s t c a r d   B o o k ™

Bishop Pass

King's River Canyon, California, 1936

by Ansel Adams (American, 1902–1984).

National Archives and Records Administration.

T h e   M u r a l   P r o j e c t
A   P o s t c a r d   B o o k ™

Rocky Mountain National Park, Never Summer Range

Colorado, 1942

by Ansel Adams (American, 1902–1984).

National Archives and Records Administration.

T h e   M u r a l   P r o j e c t

A   P o s t c a r d   B o o k ™

Old Faithful Geyser, Yellowstone National Park

Wyoming, 1942

by Ansel Adams (American, 1902–1984).

National Archives and Records Administration.

T h e   M u r a l   P r o j e c t

A   P o s t c a r d   B o o k ™

An Unnamed Peak

King's River Canyon, California, 1936

by Ansel Adams (American, 1902–1984).

National Archives and Records Administration.

T h e   M u r a l   P r o j e c t

A   P o s t c a r d   B o o k ™

In Glacier National Park

Montana, 1942

by Ansel Adams (American, 1902–1984).

National Archives and Records Administration.

T h e   M u r a l   P r o j e c t

A   P o s t c a r d   B o o k ™

The Tetons—Snake River

Grand Teton National Park, Wyoming, 1942

by Ansel Adams (American, 1902–1984).

National Archives and Records Administration

The Mural Project

A Postcard Book™